Create and Share | Thinking Digitally

Creating Slide Shows

By Ann Truesdell

Published in the United States of America by Cherry Lake Publishing Group
Ann Arbor, Michigan
www.cherrylakepublishing.com

Series Adviser: Kristin Fontichiaro
Reading Adviser: Marla Conn, MS, Ed., Literacy specialist, Read-Ability, Inc.
Book Designer: Felicia Macheske
Character Illustrator: Rachael McLean

Photo Credits: © gpointstudio/Shutterstock.com, 5; © Monkey Business Images/Shutterstock.com, 9; © Ralph Eshelman/Shutterstock.com, 11; © PR Image Factory/Shutterstock.com, 15; © myboys.me/Shutterstock.com, 21

Graphics Credits Throughout: © the simple surface/Shutterstock.com; © Diana Rich/Shutterstock.com; © lemony/Shutterstock.com; © CojoMoxon/Shutterstock.com; © IreneArt/Shutterstock.com; © Artefficient/Shutterstock.com; © Marie Nimrichterova/Shutterstock.com; © Svetolk/Shutterstock.com; © EV-DA/Shutterstock.com; © briddy/Shutterstock.com; © Mix3r/Shutterstock.com

Copyright © 2021 by Cherry Lake Publishing Group

All rights reserved. No part of this book may be reproduced or utilized in any form or by any means without written permission from the publisher.

Cherry Lake Press is an imprint of Cherry Lake Publishing Group.

Library of Congress Cataloging-in-Publication Data has been filed and is available at catalog.loc.gov

Cherry Lake Publishing Group would like to acknowledge the work of the Partnership for 21st Century Learning, a Network of Battelle for Kids. Please visit *http://www.battelleforkids.org/networks/p21* for more information.

Printed in the United States of America
Corporate Graphics

Table of CONTENTS

CHAPTER ONE
Sharing Slide Shows 4

CHAPTER TWO
Prepare to Dazzle! 8

CHAPTER THREE
Design Time 14

CHAPTER FOUR
The Finishing Touch 18

GLOSSARY 22
FOR MORE INFORMATION 23
INDEX 24
ABOUT THE AUTHOR 24

CHAPTER ONE

Sharing Slide Shows

You have some cool facts that you'd like to share. How do you get people's attention? Try a slide show!

Slides are a series of pages filled with text (words) and images, such as pictures, graphs, or charts. Some even have music and video! When you create many slides on the computer and put them in a special order, you have made a slide show.

You might use a slide show if you are planning a presentation. When you present information, you are explaining facts or ideas to an **audience**. A few words or sentences on the slides can help your audience understand what is most important. Adding images can help make your point and keep everyone interested. A slide show can help you stay on track as a presenter, too. If you forget what you were going to talk about next, just peek at your slide!

A slide show can help you share ideas and facts using both words and pictures.

Slide shows aren't always presented live. You can create a slide show for people to watch on their own. You might have your audience view the slide show at their own **pace**. Or you could set up a slide show that switches from slide to slide on its own. No matter how you choose to present your slides, the best slide shows get people interested in the ideas you are presenting.

There are many programs you can choose from to create a slide show. The most popular tools are Google Slides (which is free and available on the internet), Microsoft PowerPoint (which comes with many Windows computers), and Keynote (which comes with many Apple computers). Other tools that are online include Prezi, Haiku Deck, Buncee, VoiceThread, Pear Deck, and Animoto.

ACTIVITY

Try this:

Your teacher has asked you to present on what the Chippewa people ate. You want to tell your class this information:

The Chippewa people lived in what is now called Michigan. They ate foods that grew well on the land, such as corn, wild rice, and berries. They hunted deer, bear, moose, elk, and small animals like birds. They fished in lakes and rivers. They often made their foods into soups and stews. I think I would most enjoy their recipe for popped wild rice with berries and maple syrup.

You could say all of this when you are presenting. But it's too many words to show on a slide! Your audience will not **focus** on what you are saying if they are busy reading a paragraph. You should only highlight the most important words on your slide. How might you share these facts on a slide? You could show a simple list of these foods with a photo or two. You could include the recipe of popped wild rice with berries and maple syrup. What other ideas can you come up with?

Some slide shows are put online for people to view on their own.

CHAPTER TWO

Prepare to Dazzle!

The best slide shows are very organized. Good organization takes practice and planning. First, you should decide on the **topic** of your presentation. Next, gather your information. Write it down on a piece of paper or a computer document.

Once you have all of the information that you want to present, it's time to organize it. What information goes together? If you were presenting about the Chippewa people, you might put all of the food information together. This could be one slide. You could have another slide about their **shelter** and another slide about their clothing.

Good slide shows are entertaining and informative.

What should you write on each slide? Pick out the most important information. Don't write full paragraphs! Short sentences or phrases are good. Try to use bullet points too. This helps break up the **content** and helps your audience follow along. You want words that are large and easy to read.

People love pictures! Images can make a slide show more interesting. They can help your audience learn even more about your topic. If you talk about popped rice, will anyone know what it looks like? Show a picture!

Only include the most important information on your slides.

CHAPTER THREE

Design Time

Organizing your information and picking out important facts to share was a lot of work! Are you ready for the fun part?

It's time to **design** your slides so that they are interesting for an audience to view. Design involves picking out colors, backgrounds, **fonts**, and **layouts**. Your program will suggest some premade designs, called **templates**.

Templates give you a choice of different layouts to apply to your slides. Templates help arrange the headings, text boxes, and images in a certain order. Most programs allow you to change the template to personalize it to your presentation.

Good contrast, or differences, makes your text show up clearly.

Your goal is to create slides that make your audience's eyes go to the most important information first. You want to choose a design that you can use for most or all of your slides. Sometimes one or two slides will have a different background, font, or layout. You might do this to bring extra attention to that slide. But remember, less is more. Too many features may **distract** your audience.

Keep your slides neat and simple.

ACTIVITY

Try this:

Another part of your job as a designer is to make sure your **theme** fits the mood of your presentation. Fun, happy topics can use brighter colors and sillier fonts than serious or sad topics. Can you match the topics below with the best theme design?

Topics:

1. Cats and kittens
2. Robots
3. Planting trees for Earth Day
4. Scary stories
5. The water cycle

Themes:

a. Laser theme, high-tech design
b. Bright pink bubble fonts on a pale background
c. Green words on a white background
d. Red font on a black background
e. Dark blue fonts on a pale blue background

What did you think about when you paired the topics with the themes? How did you decide which theme would fit best?

Answers:

1: b   2: a   3: c   4: d   5: e

CHAPTER FOUR

The Finishing Touch

If you thought you were finished, think again! Most slide show programs have many additional features. They can help you grab your audience's attention and make the show more fun to watch. These finishing touches to your slide show are what make your presentation a show!

There are programs that let you put in **animations**. Some people use animations so that text appears one line at a time. This can help your audience focus on one piece of information at a time. But be careful that it is not distracting. Too much animation can confuse your audience!

Videos can also be helpful additions to slide shows. Choose only the videos that are needed. Does the video say or show things better than you could? Don't let your videos distract your audience from your information. And don't let the videos replace you as the presenter.

You can add sounds to your presentation too. You could add a simple sound to just one slide. For example, you might put in a sound to show what a healthy puppy sounds like. Or you might add some background music to set the tone for your slide show. Be careful when choosing music. Music that is too loud or has too many words can be distracting.

Don't forget to cite your sources! This means you are telling your audience where you got your information from. It is very common to have a Works Cited or Bibliography page at the end of a slide show. This is where you list all of the resources that you used. Or you might add your citations at the bottom of each slide. Citations give formal credit to an author. Pictures often include information that says who owns them and where they were found.

Transitions are the movements that happen as your slides change from one to the next. Sometimes it's fun to make it look like your slides are **dissolving** into the next slide. Or you might make it look as if someone is turning a page in a book. You may need to set up transitions where your slides automatically change from one slide to the next. You would do this when you are posting slides for others to watch without you.

These extra details can be fun and entertaining. However, too many special touches can be too much. Your audience can only focus on a few things at a time. Make sure that any finishing touches are just "touches" of fun that let your personality show. You want your information to shine through!

Animated transitions can give you and your audience time to pause and reflect as a new slide loads.

ACTIVITY

Try this:

With an adult's permission, try out one of the slide show programs mentioned in chapter 1. Make some slide shows that are just for fun! You might choose to make one about a topic you already know a lot about. Maybe you could surprise a family member by making a slide show about what makes them special.

With practice, slide shows will become easy and quick to make. Keep playing and you'll be a powerful presenter!

What would you take away from a slide to make it look less busy?

GLOSSARY

animations (an-uh-MAY-shuhnz) activities of making movies by using drawings, pictures, or computer graphics

audience (AW-dee-uhns) people who give attention to something said, done, or written

cite (SITE) to write down where your information came from

content (KAHN-tent) the words, images, and videos that you put on your slides

design (dih-ZINE) to draw a plan for something that can be made

dissolving (dih-ZAHLV-ing) when one slide disappears as the next one shows up

distract (dih-STRAKT) to take attention away from what is important

focus (FOH-kuhs) to give your attention to something or somebody

fonts (FAHNTS) styles of printed letters and numbers

layouts (LAY-outs) the arrangement of text, images, and design on a slide

pace (PASE) the speed of something

relevant (REL-uh-vuhnt) important to what is being talked about

shelter (SHEL-tur) a place that provides protection, like homes

templates (TEM-plitz) premade layouts used to create a slide show

tepee (TEE-pee) a cone-shaped tent formerly used by some Native American tribes

theme (THEEM) the colors, fonts, and designs of a slide show

topic (TAH-pik) the subject of your slide show

wigwams (WIG-wahmz) dome-shaped huts formerly used by some Native American tribes

For More INFORMATION

BOOK

Truesdell, Ann. *Creating and Sharing a Slideshow*. New York, NY: Smartbook Media Inc., 2018.

WEBSITES

Google Slides
https://www.google.com/slides
Create and share your slide show using Google Slides.

Google Slides for Kids – Episode 1
https://youtu.be/lfpneIqnXTE
Watch this informative video on how to design a slide show using Google Slides.

INDEX

animations, 18, 20
audience, 4, 6, 7, 10, 14, 16, 18

backgrounds, 14, 16

citations, 19
colors, 14, 17
contrast, 15

distractions, 16, 18, 19

fonts, 14, 16, 17

images, 4, 10, 12
information
  citing sources, 19
  gathering, 8
  organizing, 10
  presenting on slides, 16

layouts, 14, 16

mood, 17
music, 19

organization, 8

presentations, 4
programs, slide show, 6

slide shows
  creating, 8–13
  designing, 14–17
  organizing, 8
  programs, 6
  sharing, 4–7
  special features, 18–21
  sounds, 19
  sources, 19

templates, 14
theme, 14, 17
topic, 8
transitions, 20

videos, 18

About the AUTHOR

Ann Truesdell is a school librarian in Michigan. She and her husband, Mike, are the proud parents of James, Charlotte, Matilda, and Alice. They all enjoy reading, traveling, being outside, and spending time with their dog, Leia.